# John C. Frémont:

## Pathfinder of the West

Explorers of New Worlds

# John C. Frémont:

## Pathfinder of the West

Hal Marcovitz

Chelsea House Publishers
Philadelphia

Prepared for Chelsea House Publishers by:
OTTN Publishing, Stockton, N.J.

CHELSEA HOUSE PUBLISHERS
**Editor in Chief:** Sally Cheney
**Associate Editor in Chief:** Kim Shinners
**Production Manager:** Pamela Loos
**Art Director:** Sara Davis
**Director of Photography:** Judy L. Hasday
**Project Editors:** LeeAnne Gelletly, Brian Baughan
**Series Designer:** Keith Trego

First Printing
1 3 5 7 9 8 6 4 2

Library of Congress Cataloging-in-Publication Data

Marcovitz, Hal.
   John C. Frémont : pathfinder of the West / Hal
   Marcovitz.
      p. cm.–(Explorers of new worlds)
Includes bibliographical references and index.
ISBN 0-7910-6430-1 (hardcover : alk. paper) –
ISBN 0-7910-6431-X (pbk. : alk. paper)
1. Frémont, John Charles, 1813-1890–Juvenile literature.
2. Explorers–United States–Biography–Juvenile
literature. 3. Explorers–West (U.S.)–Biography–Juvenile
literature. 4. West (U.S.)–Discovery and exploration–
Juvenile literature. 5. Generals–United States–
Biography–Juvenile literature. 6. Presidential
candidates–United States–Biography–Juvenile
literature. 7. United States–Territorial expansion–
Juvenile literature. [1. Frémont, John Charles, 1813-1890.
2. Explorers. 3. West (U.S.)–Discovery and
exploration.] I. Title. II. Series.

E415.9.F8 M37 2001
973.6'092–dc21
[B]                                        2001028299

# Contents

"I Sprang upon the Summit . . ."

Explorers of New Worlds

*Frémont Peak rises above the Wyoming landscape. The mountain is named for John C. Frémont, who climbed it while mapping trails throughout the American West in 1842.*

I

By 1842, Christopher "Kit" Carson had already earned a reputation as an American frontier hero. He was a hunter, trapper, expert horseman, and scout. He would later become a soldier, serving his country in the Mexican War and then the Civil War.

But on a late July morning in 1842, Carson was uncharacteristically frightened. For weeks, he had been waiting at Fort Laramie, Wyoming, for John Charles Frémont to catch up with him. Frémont, the leader of the westward-traveling expedition to which Carson belonged, had taken a different route so that he could map sites for future army outposts.

As Carson waited for Frémont, he heard bad news about the road ahead. Sioux Indian warriors were said to be attacking settlers. The Cheyenne and Gros Ventre Indians were also believed to be hostile. When Frémont finally reached Fort Laramie, Carson shared his concerns with his leader.

Frémont insisted that the expedition continue. Kit Carson reluctantly agreed to stay on as Frémont's guide, but before leaving Fort Laramie, Carson made out his last will and testament.

Frémont's expedition of 23 adventurers left Fort Laramie on July 21. As they inched their way westward toward the Rocky Mountains, they encountered no trouble from the Indians. Indeed, they occasionally crossed paths with solitary Cheyenne warriors, who seemed hungry and frightened themselves. The Cheyennes told Frémont that the land ahead was barren and had been ravaged by locusts. Frémont and his men would later write off the Cheyennes' warnings as tall tales.

On August 8, they found the South Pass. This

*Native Americans called Kit Carson "Rope Thrower" because of his skill with a lasso. The frontier scout became famous because of his association with explorer John C. Frémont in the 1840s.*

was a passageway through the Wind River Mountain range, one of several western ranges that compose the Rocky Mountains. Locating the South Pass–a wide, flat opening through the mountains some 8,000 feet above sea level–had been a prime goal of Frémont's mission. After making it through the pass, Frémont and his men came upon a breathtakingly beautiful mountain. It rose 13,730 feet into the crisp, blue Wyoming sky.

The mountain stood in a wilderness of rough, rocky terrain. Near its base, the explorers found the source of three great rivers: the Wind River, which flows east to the Mississippi; the Green River, which flows south to the Colorado River; and the Gros Ventre River, which flows north to the Columbia River. The explorers made careful notes, because their mission involved making maps of the terrain they explored.

Frémont decided to climb the mountain. He took four men along for the ascent, one of whom was Charles Preuss, a professional mapmaker and long-time friend who would accompany Frémont on future missions.

Preuss wrote about the harrowing climb up the mountain. "With the first steps I could dig my heels into the snow; then it became harder," he recalled. "I slipped, sat down on my pants and slid downhill at a great speed. Although I made all efforts to hold back by trying to dig my fingers into the icy crust, I slid down about 200 feet, until the bare rocks stopped me again."

And later, he grumbled, "No supper, no break-fast, little or no sleep—who can enjoy climbing a mountain under these circumstances?"

But Frémont had a much different recollection of the events on that magnificent summer day in 1842. Readers of Frémont's account find a man thrilled with the adventure and eager to explore onward, yet also filled with a sense of awe as he witnessed nature's grandeur from high atop a peak in the Rocky Mountains.

He wrote: "I sprang upon the summit, and another step would have precipitated me into an immense snowfield 500 feet below. . . . Here, on the summit, where the stillness and solitude [were] complete, we thought ourselves beyond the region of animated life; but while we were sitting on the rock, a solitary bee came winging his flight from the eastern valley and lit on the knee of one of the men.

"It was a strange place, the icy rock and the highest peak of the Rocky Mountains, for a lover of warm sunshine and flowers. We pleased ourselves with the idea that we were the first of our species to cross the mountain barrier–solitary pioneers to foretell the advance of civilization."

The expedition was a success. Frémont and his men descended from the mountain and turned back east, their mission accomplished. The huge and icy mountain behind them in the heart of Wyoming would come to be known as Frémont Peak.

*John C. Frémont as a young man in his U.S. Army uniform. In 1838, Frémont became a mapmaker with the U.S. Army's Corps of Topographical Engineers. This position would launch his career as an explorer of the West.*

# The Pathfinder

# 2

I n 1813, two men who would have much to do with shaping the future of the United States found themselves sharing rooms in a hotel in Nashville, Tennessee.

One of the men was Andrew Jackson, who was leading a *contingent* of troops from Tennessee fighting in the War of 1812. Jackson and his rifle-toting soldiers had just spent several weary months in Mississippi. They had seen no action against the British, so Jackson decided to march them 800 miles home to Tennessee. Later, Jackson and his riflemen would see considerable action. Jackson, who was known as "Old Hickory," emerged from the War of 1812 a hero. At the Battle of New Orleans, he led the Americans in a decisive victory over the British. He would eventually launch a political career and go on to be elected president in 1828.

The other man at the hotel was Thomas Hart Benton, head of one of the **regiments** under Jackson's command. After the war, Benton moved to Missouri and won election to the U.S. Senate, where he reigned as a leader in Congress for 30 years.

The two men would later become political allies, championing the cause of "**Manifest Destiny**"–the belief that Americans should push their young nation's borders as far west as the shores of the Pacific Ocean. But on this night in Nashville, Jackson and Benton were hardly on friendly terms. Relations between the two soldiers had been strained for months. Benton's brother, Jesse, who was also staying in the hotel that night, had fought a man in a **duel**–an agreed-upon combat, with pistols, engaged in by two gentlemen as a way of resolving a dispute. Dueling has long been outlawed in the United States and other nations, but in the wild years of the early 1800s, the practice was common. Jesse Benton survived the duel but made no friends with Andy Jackson, who sided with the other man.

*Andrew Jackson, a hero of the War of 1812, would become the seventh president of the United States. During his two terms (1829-1837), Jackson encouraged the migration of American settlers into western lands.*

In the Nashville hotel, the feud between Old Hickory and the Bentons finally reached the boiling point. The Bentons went after Jackson with a bull-whip, knives, and pistols. They destroyed the lobby of the hotel. One of Thomas Benton's shots struck Jackson in the shoulder. Another shot went through the wall of one of the hotel's rooms. Staying in the room was the family of Charles Fremon, a French immigrant. When the shot pierced the wall, it narrowly missed a sleeping baby. That was Charles's son, John Charles. Charles Fremon swung open the door of the room, strode into the lobby, and commanded the feuding soldiers to put down their weapons. The Bentons meekly complied. So did a wounded and bleeding Andrew Jackson.

It was a strange coincidence. The two men who would be instrumental in directing the country's Manifest Destiny found themselves feuding in a hotel where the young boy who would carry out their wishes slept soundly in his crib.

⸝⸍⸝⸍⸝⸍⸝

In 1845, newspaper editor John L. O'Sullivan first used the term Manifest Destiny, thus putting words to a desire many Americans had harbored since the end of the War of 1812. During the first half of the 18th century, the nation's borders hardly resembled the continental United States of the present day. Most of America's population lived east of the Mississippi River. Indeed, the land west of the Mississippi was untamed, rugged, and mysterious. Most of the region was contained in unchartered territories; the westernmost state at the time, Texas, didn't join the Union until 1845.

Over the years, other countries had regarded much of the West as their property. The Louisiana Purchase, which contained territory from the Gulf of Mexico to the Canadian border, was bought from

France by President Thomas Jefferson in 1803. Well into the 1840s, Mexico claimed ownership of vast regions of the American Southwest–an area that now includes Utah, New Mexico, and California. Even Russian pioneers making their way across Alaska and then down from Canada settled in California and raised their nation's flag there. Another disputed region was the Oregon Territory, which the British regarded as their own. And certainly the Indians–who were, after all, in America first–felt they had rights to the land.

That didn't sit well with American citizens or their political leaders. Many people were willing to fight anyone standing in the way of expansion, whether they were Mexicans, Indians, or Englishmen.

In 1819, President James Monroe had sent 2,000 U.S. soldiers led by Andrew Jackson into Florida, which

**"Nothing upon Earth can be farther from the genius and principles of this Republic than the acquisition of territory by military conquest," wrote John O'Sullivan in his newspaper, the *New York Morning News*. He went on to say that if England wanted another fight on its hands over disputed territory, America was ready to fight "by right of our manifest destiny."**

*Missouri senator Thomas Hart Benton was an influential advocate of Manifest Destiny during the mid-19th century. Benton's motivation was partly economic—he wanted to increase U.S. trade with China—but Benton also saw western lands as a place where poor immigrants could prosper as farmers.*

at the time was owned by Spain. Jackson captured the Spanish fort of Saint Marks virtually without resistance, then seized the port of Pensacola. He replaced Pensacola's Spanish governor with one of his own colonels. Spanish leaders were upset, but they backed down rather than risk war with the United States. Spain **ceded** Florida to the United States, and in 1821 Andrew Jackson was named the first territorial governor of Florida, a position he held briefly.

Jackson's contributions to the expansion of the United States would continue after his election as president in 1828. He signed the Indian Removal Act, which authorized the relocation of any tribe east of the Mississippi River to lands in the West. Thousands of Native Americans were forced off their forested and fertile lands and made to live on the unfamiliar plains of Oklahoma. When some Cheyennes rose up and threatened to fight back, Jackson sent in the U.S. Army.

He had a willing ally in the U.S. Senate in his old adversary Thomas Hart Benton. However, Senator Benton had the vision to see that conquering the untamed land west of the Mississippi was not enough. Americans had to be convinced to settle there. The young nation needed somebody to trek out into the wilderness to mark the old trails, some of which hadn't been revisited since Lewis and Clark made their way west in the first years of the 19th century. Somebody would have to find new trails west, including the elusive South Pass through Wyoming's Wind River Mountains.

What's more, Benton wanted somebody to put into words the wonders that would be seen and experienced by the settlers as they made their way to the Pacific coast. He wanted his author to use colorful language so that people in the east who read about the new lands would become excited enough to want to live there.

In addition, Benton knew the settlers would need maps. Essentially, he believed, the United States needed a pathfinder.

❧❧❧❧❧

John Charles Frémont was born in Savannah, Georgia, on January 21, 1813. His father was Charles Fremon, a French **aristocrat** who fled his country during the French Revolution. From 1789 to 1792, many aristocrats–people born to wealth–were rounded up and killed at the **guillotine** by peasants who had overthrown the monarchy and established the French Republic. To avoid losing his head in the guillotine, Fremon sailed for the United States.

After arriving in Virginia, Fremon learned how to make cabinets. He also met Ann Whiting, the daughter of a wealthy Virginia family. Ann left her husband to run off with Charles. When their son John was born, Ann and Charles had not yet married.

They eventually settled in Charleston, South Carolina. Charles Fremon started spelling his name "Frémont," thinking it more Americanized. Three other children were soon born to the Frémonts. But in 1818, when John was five, his father died.

Ann bought a boardinghouse in Charleston, and for the next several years she managed to eke out a living. Certainly, there wasn't enough money to guarantee a good education for young John. While growing up in Charleston, however, John started running errands for John W. Mitchell, a prosperous lawyer who grew fond of the fatherless boy. Mitchell agreed to pay for John's education.

When John turned 14, he enrolled in Charleston College, an exclusive school for young men in South Carolina. An eager learner, he soon came to the attention of Dr. Charles Robertson, the school's headmaster. "It seemed to me that young Frémont learned as if by mere intuition," Robertson later wrote of the student. "I myself was utterly astonished and at the same time delighted with his progress. I could not help liking him greatly."

John was particularly good at mathematics. In fact, he soon knew as much math as his teachers, and Robertson had to hire a professional mathematician to tutor the boy.

He may have impressed teachers with his math skills, but Frémont seemed to have little interest in most other subjects. Eventually, he dropped out of Charleston College before receiving a diploma.

Still, the time he spent at Charleston College did not go to waste. One day, Frémont attended a lecture at the college given by Joel R. Poinsett. Frémont asked Poinsett so many thoughtful questions that Poinsett couldn't help but be impressed with the young student. Poinsett and Frémont became instant friends, and Poinsett eventually became a major influence in the young man's life.

Poinsett had been a U.S. ambassador to Mexico as well as a physician, lawyer, and adventurer. He had crossed the Atlantic in a clipper ship and toured Europe. When Frémont left Charleston College in 1833, Poinsett found him a job aboard the *Natchez,* a naval ship headed for South America. Frémont's job would be to teach math to young navy midshipmen. Frémont spent two years aboard the *Natchez,* visiting exotic ports in South America and exploring the leafy Amazon wilderness.

**Joel Poinsett's name would become familiar to garden lovers worldwide: an amateur *botanist*, he would have the honor of seeing a plant, the poinsettia, named in his honor. The poinsettia is the bright red flower commonly seen as a centerpiece on dinner tables around Christmas time.**

When he returned, Frémont found himself aching for the explorer's life. He found it in 1838 by joining the U.S. Army's Corps of Topographical Engineers. In 1838 and 1839, Frémont participated in two mapmaking expeditions along the Missouri and Mississippi Rivers under the leadership of Joseph Nicholas Nicollet.

Nicollet was an expert mapmaker as well as a seasoned explorer. He taught Frémont not only the techniques of ***topography***, but also skills for living in the wilderness. By 1841, Frémont was regarded as a bright star of the Topographical Engineers, and greater adventures lay ahead.

# The Oregon Trail

*Immigrants move west along the Oregon Trail in this Currier and Ives lithograph from 1865. It was up to Frémont to create a good map of the route that would open the American West to expansion in the second half of the 19th century.*

3

For more than 400,000 Americans, the way west meant a long and dangerous journey by wagon train over the Oregon Trail. The 2,000-mile-long trail cut a rugged path through prairies, forests, mountains, and swamps. It stretched from Independence, Missouri, to the Columbia River in present-day Oregon. But it was never a clearly defined road. Prairie schooners–covered wagons based on the design of Conestoga wagons used in colonial days–often traveled miles apart, the trail changing course whenever storms washed out pathways, snowdrifts proved too deep for the pack animals, or rivers seemed too dangerous to cross.

Nevertheless, land was available out west–a seemingly endless supply of land for *homesteaders* anxious to escape the poverty of America's eastern cities. And many people were quite willing to

## Lewis and Clark

Parts of the Oregon Trail had been explored as early as 1804 and 1805 when Meriwether Lewis (right) and William Clark (below) made their way west on an expedition to explore the Louisiana Purchase, a vast area of North America purchased from the French in 1803. Lewis and Clark had reached the Pacific Ocean and returned, but they traveled much of the way in canoes– hardly a fitting mode of travel for pioneer families who would need to tote all their possessions.

endure the dangers and drudgeries of pioneer life for this treasure at the end of the trail. Clearly, though, a good map of the Oregon Trail was needed before the true migration west could begin.

Senator Thomas Hart Benton convinced his fellow members of Congress to appropriate $30,000 to outfit a team of explorers, who would make their way west as far as the South Pass in Wyoming. The job of putting together the expedition fell to the U.S. Army Bureau of Topographical Engineers, the army's chief mapmakers. And to lead the expedition, the army picked a young lieutenant–John C. Frémont. His selection was no coincidence. Benton made sure Frémont won the appointment.

Frémont would probably have come to Benton's attention simply on the reputation he had earned as one of the army's most skilled mapmakers. But Frémont was well known to Benton for another reason: he had married the senator's daughter.

John Frémont and Jessie Benton had **eloped**. He was 28; she was 17. At first, the senator was angry, but eventually his heart softened and he grew fond of his son-in-law. And so in 1842, Benton didn't have to search far for the man who would lead the first mapmaking expedition over the Oregon Trail.

Actually, Frémont had other friends in high places as well. Joel Poinsett, who had found Frémont the job aboard the *Natchez,* was appointed secretary of war in 1837 and served in that post until shortly before Frémont's Oregon Trail expedition left Missouri. In the 1800s, the secretary of war was the civilian head of the U.S. Army. (Today, the secretary of defense has this responsibility.)

John Frémont, Kit Carson, and the others in the ***corps*** of explorers left St. Louis, Missouri, in May 1842. They stopped briefly in Westport, Missouri, which is now Kansas City. On June 10, the expedition set out in search of the South Pass.

The travelers could cover 25 or 30 miles in a day, depending on the terrain and weather. When heavy storms on the prairies turned the trail to mud, the explorers' progress was considerably slowed. Rivers were difficult to cross and accidents were not unusual. On one unfortunate day, the expedition lost its entire supply of coffee and sugar. On many days, boredom reigned, and the unchanging trail seemed endless.

Frémont usually found himself busy, though. Using a telescope, he made careful astronomical observations, noting the positions of the stars and

*Jesse Benton was 17 when she ran away to marry John Charles Frémont. During their 49 years together, Jessie helped her husband write books about his adventures on the western trails. This portrait of Jesse was painted in 1856.*

planets. He used a **sextant** and **chronometer** to determine longitude and latitude–the parallel north-south and east-west lines on maps that identify specific locations on the earth. Charles Preuss, who had accompanied Frémont on other missions, was responsible for sketching landmarks such as mountains and river forks, and making note of them on the expedition's maps.

The corps followed the Platte River through present-day Nebraska; when the explorers reached a fork in the Platte, Frémont took a small group south to search for sites for future army outposts. He sent Carson north with the rest of the men with orders to wait for him in Fort Laramie.

While making his way to Fort Laramie, Frémont expressed some doubts of his own about the trail ahead. Like Carson, he had heard reports of hostile Indians, and although the explorers had encountered friendly Indians on the trail from time to time, Frémont worried that their luck wouldn't hold.

"Daily, several people, white and Indian, have been killed in the country lying to the west of us," Frémont wrote in his journal on July 9. "If our party cannot be increased at Fort Laramie it would be best to turn back and limit ourselves to the survey of the Platte River. It would be ridiculous to risk the lives of 23 people just to determine a few longitudes and latitudes and to find out the height of the mountain range. The men are not at all inclined to continue without reinforcements. In a few days everything will be settled at Laramie. I hope we shall get that far safely."

Frémont did make it to Fort Laramie, where he met up with Kit Carson and the other members of the corps. Carson expressed similar fears about the road ahead, but Frémont made the decision to push on. On August 8 they found the South Pass and

*In the mid-1840s, Fort Laramie, Wyoming, was an important stopping point for settlers traveling west.*

climbed what would later be called Frémont Peak. Frémont and his party then turned back to St. Louis.

But making the trip and drawing maps was only half the job. Benton insisted that Frémont put down in writing all that he had seen. The senator wanted others to read those words and be convinced to make the journey west themselves.

At first, Frémont tried to write the report himself. He complained, though, that "the horseback life" hardly suited him to "the indoor work of writing." For days, Frémont agonized over the ***manuscript***,

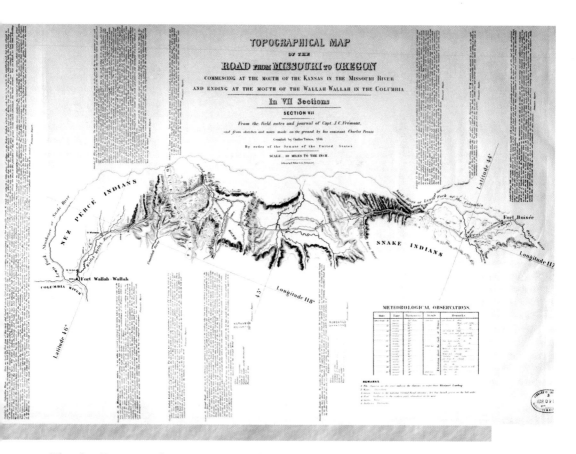

*Charles Preuss, who accompanied Frémont on several of his expeditions, made this map of the Oregon Trail. It includes detailed notes about the region, as well as a chart giving information about weather conditions.*

unable to put his thoughts into writing. Finally, he turned to his wife. Jessie and John Frémont worked together on the book: he told her what he saw, and she described it in words people could understand.

The result of their efforts was a highly readable 207-page report about life on the trail, peppered with tales of buffalo hunts, encounters with Indians, and struggles against nature. The Frémonts were careful to weave into the account accurate descriptions of the plant and animal life in the West. The report, presented to Congress on March 2, 1843, was titled "A Report of an Exploration of the Country Lying Between the Missouri River and the Rocky Mountains on the Line of the Kansas and Great Platte Rivers." Senator Benton was delighted, and Congress ordered 1,000 copies printed for sale to the public. All were quickly sold.

For the most part, the report sent the message that Thomas Hart Benton had desired when he dispatched Frémont into the wilderness: that people seeking to establish farms could find valuable land in the west.

"The soil of all this country is excellent, admirably adapted to agricultural purposes, and would support a large population," wrote Frémont.

The success of the report helped Frémont earn a reputation as one of America's great explorers. It also helped him earn a nickname. From that point on, John C. Frémont would be known as "the Pathfinder."

# "Rock upon
# Rock"

*During his second expedition to the West, Frémont explored the Great Salt Lake, located in the present-day state of Utah.*

4

*I*f Frémont thought he would have time to enjoy his new status as a celebrity and American hero, he was quite mistaken. Congress wanted more of the Oregon Territory mapped and explored, so Frémont was once again dispatched to lead a corps of explorers west.

The plan for the second expedition was to take the Oregon Trail as far west as the Columbia River in the present-day state of Oregon. This time, Frémont and his men would travel the entire length of the Oregon Trail. They would start in Independence, Missouri, and proceed along the Missouri River to the Platte River, which they would follow into the Rocky Mountains. After making their way through the South Pass, they would follow the Snake River to the Columbia Valley in Oregon.

Frémont enlisted 25 men and prepared to leave Westport, Missouri, in May 1843. Preuss and Carson signed up for another adventure with Frémont.

By late August of 1843, the explorers had reached the South Pass. On September 6, they found themselves at the shores of the Great Salt Lake in present-day Utah. The Great Salt Lake is one of America's most unusual natural features. A huge inland lake some 1,700 square miles in size, it is—as its name implies—composed of salt water. The salt is carried into the lake by its *tributaries*, the Jordan, Weaver, and Bear Rivers, but no river carries water out of the lake. That's why the lake remains salty: water is lost through evaporation, but the salt stays behind in the lake.

Some of Frémont's men believed the Great Salt Lake contained mystical powers. "Among the trappers, including those in my own camp, were many who believed that somewhere in its surface was a terrible whirlpool, through which the waters found their way to the ocean through some underground cave," wrote Frémont.

Frémont himself had a different opinion. He wrote that his arrival at the Great Salt Lake was "one of the great points of the exploration. . . . As we looked eagerly over the lake in the first emotions of excited pleasure, I am doubtful if the followers of Balboa felt more enthusiasm when . . . they saw for the first time the great western ocean." (Vasco Núñez de Balboa, a 16th century Spanish explorer, was the first European to see the Pacific Ocean.)

**Frémont was not the first man to see the Great Salt Lake. European trappers and missionaries had made note of the body of water in their journals as far back as the 1770s. And of course the Native Americans of the area were familiar with the lake.**

The Pathfinder decided to explore the Great Salt Lake, and he had brought along a fairly new invention for just such a task: a rubber raft. As with many untested new inventions, however, the raft had its problems. "Two of the air cylinders leaked so much that one man had to remain at the bellows all the time in order to keep them full of air to support the boat," Frémont wrote.

From the Great Salt Lake, the corps turned north and marched 100 miles to Fort Hill, located along the Snake River in present-day Idaho. It was a weary, dispirited group that made camp at the fort. Some of the men had grown edgy during the exploration of the Great Salt Lake. They found this huge body of salt water, and the land around it, eerie. Miles and miles of barren, rocky countryside stretched along the water in a region Frémont would later name the Great Basin.

**The Great Basin is the vast area of the United States between the Wasatch Mountains to the east and the Sierra Nevada Mountains to the west. It contains most of present-day Nevada along with parts of California, Idaho, Utah, Wyoming, and Oregon.**

What's more, food was scarce. During their march through the Great Basin, the men were forced to kill seagulls for food, or to try to make meals out of the sparse grasses and roots they found.

Conditions at Fort Hill weren't that much better. Supplies were short at the outpost and Frémont was unable to buy fresh horses.

Then the expedition found itself bogged down when an unexpected ice storm hit the region. Many members of the corps urged Frémont to turn back. The Pathfinder wouldn't hear of it, although he gave his men permission to return on their own. Eleven members of the corps elected to head for home.

After leaving Fort Hill, the men who remained with the expedition followed the Snake River through a rugged landscape of sagebrush and lava boulders that Frémont characterized as a "melancholy and strange-looking country—one of fracture, violence and fire." Even though it was still late September, nighttime temperatures dropped below freezing. By late October, the corps emerged from the rocky terrain near present-day Walla Walla, Washington. After a few more days on the trail, the explorers reached the goal they had set out to find some 2,000 miles earlier—the Columbia River.

"The river is, indeed, a noble object, and has here attained its full magnitude," Frémont wrote.

Although the men had reached the primary objective of the mission, morale was once again low. There were few trees along this stretch of the Columbia, which made it hard to find firewood. Food was hard to find as well.

Frémont obtained a 30-foot canoe from some Indians, and the corps headed downriver. After three days of travel, they arrived at Fort Vancouver in Washington. There they rested up and Frémont made a decision: instead of returning to Missouri by way of the Oregon Trail, which had been the original plan, they would head south to further explore the Great Basin.

They left on November 25. Travel was slow; the corps was able to cover just seven or eight miles a day. Then, in present-day western Nevada—with the Sierra Nevada Mountains to the west and the flatlands of the Great Basin to the east—the corps made camp near the Carson River, just south of Pyramid Lake. While Frémont planned the next stage of the mission, Preuss and others grumbled. "We've been sitting for three days, wrapped in fog, on a miserable plateau surrounded by bare hills," Preuss wrote in his diary. "The animals are dying one after the other. Very little grass, snow instead of water."

Frémont briefly considered spending the winter at Pyramid Lake. Instead he decided to travel over the Sierra Nevada Mountains into California.

Frémont undoubtedly had Manifest Destiny on his mind when he steered his exploration west. In

1844, California was the property of Mexico. Relations between Mexico and the United States had been strained for years. In fact, the two countries were slowly moving toward war. Now, a mapmaking expedition sponsored by the U.S. Army was preparing to venture onto Mexican soil.

The trek toward California would not be an easy journey. It was wintertime, and conditions in the high Sierra Nevada Mountains were harsh. The travelers would encounter icy paths, blinding snowstorms, and bone-chilling winds. On the trail, they met a Washo Indian. When they told him of their plans to cross the mountains in winter, the Indian urged them to turn back.

"Rock upon rock . . . rock upon rock . . . snow upon snow . . . snow upon snow," the Indian told Frémont. "Even if you get over the snow, you will not be able to get down from the mountains."

On February 6, Carson and Frémont found a path through the Sierra Nevada Mountains. The corps trudged through–hungry, footsore, and cold. "The snow is terribly deep, and we can make only a few miles every day," wrote Preuss. "I am almost barefoot. This surpasses every discomfort that I have experienced so far. Here, a buffalo hide is spread on the snow—that is my feather bed."

The corps proved the Washo Indian wrong; they found the path improving as they descended from the mountains on the California side. By now, the season was also changing. On March 4, they made camp on the shores of the Sacramento River. "The associated beauties of scenery made so strong an impression on us that we have given it the name 'Beautiful Camp,'" Frémont wrote.

A few weeks later, they made their way to Sutter's Fort, a trading post just north of San Francisco.

It was time to return home. But rather than risk another crossing of the Sierra Nevada, Frémont elected to head south, forging a path through the easier terrain of the San Joaquin Valley just below San Francisco. Heading down the coast, the explorers found the Mojave River, then turned east and marched through the Mojave Desert. Five months later, the journey ended in Missouri.

Once again, John and Jessie Frémont worked together on the report of the expedition. And once again, their report was accepted enthusiastically by Congress, which ordered 10,000 copies printed and sold to the public. The most significant discovery noted in the report was Frémont's conclusion that

*A view of Sutter's Mill, California, where gold was discovered in 1848 by James Marshall. Frémont visited the area during his travels in California, and his maps and reports encouraged settlers to move west and claim land.*

the Great Basin ended short of the Pacific coast. But the report also talked about the dangerous crossing of the Sierra Nevada Mountains as well as the rolling, fertile landscape and pleasurable climate the explorers found once they reached California.

Thousands of Americans wanted to learn more about this vast territory that composed most of the continent's west coast. Soon the Pathfinder would supply the answers.

# The Bear Flag
# Rebellion

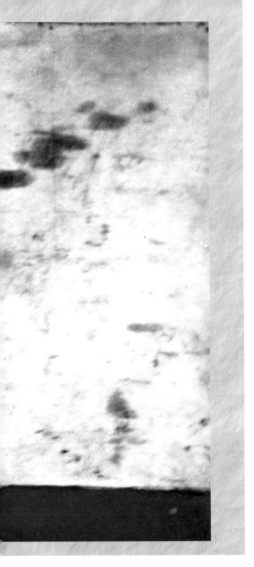

*American settlers in California, who called themselves Osos, declared their independence from Mexico in 1846. This is actually a replica of the Osos' flag; it was made after the original California Bear Flag was lost in the San Francisco earthquake of 1906.*

5

n 1540, a group of explorers under the leadership of *conquistador* Francisco Vásquez de Coronado first ventured into California, claiming the vast region for Spain. It was a grand prize for the Spanish king: 159,000 square miles of fertile land, imposing mountains, and coastal valleys.

But by the late 18th century, Spain had done little to exploit California's great natural treasures. A few priests established missions to bring Christianity to the Indians, and a handful of unlucky soldiers found themselves assigned to lonely outposts deep in California's wilderness. In 1821, Mexico won its independence from Spain and claimed California as its own. Spain didn't protest.

Meanwhile, in Washington, the fervor for Manifest Destiny continued to build. In 1835, President Andrew Jackson made an offer to Mexico to buy the San Francisco Bay. The Mexicans refused. Seven years later, President John Tyler dangled some offers for California in front of the Mexicans, but the negotiations never progressed past the talking stages.

When President James K. Polk took office in March 1845, he set the acquisition of California as a primary goal for his administration. By now, there was a tiny population of Americans living in California: about 400 settlers had found their way through the Sierra Nevada Mountains and established homesteads in northern California.

Others also had designs on California. Russian fur traders had established an outpost on the San Francisco Bay. British and French warships were regularly seen in San Francisco Bay as well as other California ports. So in December 1845, when

*During his presidential campaign in 1844, James K. Polk promised to expand U.S. territory. After annexing Texas and settling a dispute with Great Britain over the Oregon boundary, Polk turned his attention toward gaining California and other land from Mexico— either by a negotiated treaty or through a war.*

Frémont and 62 well-armed men showed up in the Santa Clara Valley near San Francisco Bay, it was clear that on this mission, the Pathfinder's job involved more than just drawing maps.

Mexico and the United States had been moving slowly toward war since 1836, when Texans won their independence from Mexico. When the United States recognized Texas as an independent republic, U.S.-Mexican relations became strained. In 1845, the United States **annexed** Texas, which soon became a state. In Washington, political leaders wanted to take still more territory from Mexican control: the New Mexico territory (which included the present-day states Nevada and Utah, as well as parts of Colorado, Arizona, New Mexico, and Wyoming) and California.

By now, Frémont was a lieutenant colonel in the U.S. Army. In June 1845, he was once again dispatched to explore a western trail. This time, he was ordered to survey the lands along the Arkansas and Red Rivers in the Oklahoma-Texas region. But Frémont was also told to carry out his mission as far west as he deemed appropriate. Frémont recruited 62 frontiersmen for the mission, including several men who had accompanied him on the first two expeditions. Kit Carson, for one, would be making another trip west under the Pathfinder's leadership.

Frémont complied with his orders, making maps of the two rivers. But after completing that job, he continued west. Once again, Frémont and his men marched across the Great Basin. The expedition crossed the Sierra Nevada Mountains in early December–this time, just beating the heavy snows– and in February they arrived at the San Joaquin Valley just below San Francisco.

They found themselves walking into a bubbling cauldron of suspicion and hostility. The Mexicans were nervous about the appearance of a U.S. Army expedition camping on their territory. The local Indians were hostile. Even the American settlers who had established homesteads in California were suspicious of Frémont's intentions.

Frémont stirred the cauldron to a boil when he started meeting with Thomas Larkin, the chief U.S. diplomat in California, in the coastal town of Monterey. José Castro, the Mexican military governor of California, suspected that Frémont and Larkin were planning an attack. Castro summoned Frémont and told him to get out of California.

The Pathfinder refused. Instead, he ordered his men to build a log fort on Hawk's Peak, just north of Monterey. In March 1846, Frémont and his men raised the Stars and Stripes over the fort, declaring the territory the property of the United States.

Castro responded by moving his own troops into position around the fort. A battle seemed likely, but tempers cooled when Larkin stepped in and assured the nervous Mexicans that Frémont had no hostile intentions. The American flag was lowered, and Frémont led his troops down the mountain. He decided to make for the safety of the trading post at Sutter's Fort to the north.

*U.S. troops storm Mexico City during the 1846 war with Mexico. The United States gained more than 500,000 square miles of territory, including California, through peace negotiations with Mexico.*

When Frémont and his men returned to the area in June, they met up with a group of about 30 hunters, trappers, and settlers who called themselves the Osos. (Oso is the Spanish word for bear.) At Frémont's urging, the Osos planned to attack a Mexican garrison camped in the Sonoma Valley north of San Francisco. The Osos made their strike in the predawn hours of June 14, and the fight was over in minutes. The Osos had surprised the ill-prepared Mexicans, who quickly surrendered.

The Osos declared California an independent republic. Somebody hastily stitched a crude white-and-red flag featuring a star, the figure of a bear, and the words "California Republic" in black letters. (Today, the state flag of California is based on the Bear Flag design.)

Just as the Osos were raising the Bear Flag over their new republic, a U.S. Navy warship under the command of Commodore Robert Stockton arrived at Monterey. Meanwhile, a U.S. Army division under the leadership of General Stephen Kearny marched into the Sonoma Valley from the south. Frémont stepped in and convinced the Osos to take orders from him. The Pathfinder now declared himself commander of the California Battalion of the U.S. Army.

Soon Mexico and the United States would be fighting a full-fledged war, which Mexico would lose. Afterward, the United States would annex California and the New Mexico territory, satisfying the desires of its people and their leaders to fulfill their Manifest Destiny. The country's borders would be pushed to the far ends of the continent. And within two years of the Bear Flag Rebellion, 100,000 American settlers would be living in California.

*In 1856, John C. Frémont became the first presidential candidate for a new political party—the Republican Party. Though he lost the election to James Buchanan, four years later a Republican would win the presidency.*

# Candidate, Abolitionist, and General 6

or John C. Frémont, the years that followed were filled with new adventures and new challenges. There were new triumphs, but there were also many disappointments.

It did not take long after the Bear Flag Rebellion for Frémont's life to change dramatically. He became caught in a power struggle between General Kearny and Commodore Stockton, both of whom felt they had the right to command the military forces in California. Frémont chose to take his orders from Stockton, which angered Kearny. It turned out that Kearny had indeed been granted complete authority in California by General Winfield Scott, commander of the U.S. Army. Frémont returned to Washington, where he was **court-martialed** for mutiny. A military court found Frémont guilty, but President Polk pardoned him and offered to restore him to the rank of lieutenant colonel. Frémont angrily refused, and resigned from the army.

For now, Frémont was through with the army but not through with exploring. In 1848, private investors hired him to survey a route for a railroad that would stretch from St. Louis to the Pacific Ocean. Frémont decided to survey the route across the Rocky Mountains in midwinter. That decision turned out to be a terrible mistake. By December, Frémont and his 22 men, hungry and frostbitten, were forced to turn back. By the time the expedition stumbled into a trading post in Taos, New Mexico, on February 12, 1849, a total of 10 men had died.

Frémont decided to give up exploration. "It needs strong enticements to undergo the hardships and denial of this kind of life," he wrote, "and as I find I have these no longer, I will drop into a quiet life."

John and Jessie Frémont made their home in San Francisco. By now, they were wealthy. Gold had been discovered on land they owned, and their fortune was valued at $10 million.

Meanwhile, California had entered the Union in 1850, and Frémont was asked to serve as one of the new state's first senators. He held that job briefly, losing an election after a year in office when proslavery leaders gained control of California politics. Frémont was a staunch **abolitionist**, a person opposed to slavery. As the decade of the 1850s dawned, the issue of slavery became more and more controversial, creating angry debates throughout the United States.

In 1856, a new political party rose up to challenge the long-established power of the Democrats. The Republicans were formed to oppose slavery. Frémont's fierce opposition to slavery in California came to the attention of the new party's leaders, and they asked him to run for president. Frémont campaigned hard, but he lost a close election to Democrat James Buchanan.

Frémont returned to California, but not for long. After the 1860 election of the Republican party's presidential candidate, Abraham Lincoln, the Southern states **seceded** from the Union, causing the outbreak of the Civil War. President Lincoln asked

*President Lincoln (left) confers with advisors and*
*generals early in the Civil War. Next to Lincoln are*
*William Henry Seward, Winfield Scott, Simon*
*Cameron, George McClellan, Benjamin Butler, John*
*Wool, Robert Anderson, John C. Frémont, and John Dix.*

Frémont to return to the military and take command
of the Union's western armies. Frémont was given
the rank of major general and ordered to defeat the
Confederate, or Southern, forces in Missouri.

Frémont was not an effective wartime general,
and the men under his command lost two decisive
battles. Then he ordered that all the property of
Confederates in Missouri be confiscated and their

slaves freed. That decision angered Lincoln. In two years Lincoln would issue the Emancipation Proclamation, declaring all the slaves in rebellious states freed. But at this stage in the conflict, the president feared Frémont's act would anger people in the Northern states who had not yet accepted the Civil War as a conflict to end slavery. Lincoln was forced to remove Frémont from command.

Later in the war Frémont served as commander of the Union armies in West Virginia, but a series of losses eventually forced Lincoln to turn over Frémont's troops to another general. Frémont resigned from the army in 1862. He sat out the rest of the war in New York City.

Later, he lost his fortune by making investments in railroads that failed. Still, the Frémonts managed to live comfortably on the money that Jessie earned writing books.

In 1890, Congress granted the Pathfinder a military **pension**, but he wouldn't live long enough to enjoy it. On July 13 of that year, while visiting friends in New York, John C. Frémont fell ill and died. He was 77 years old.

It is said that he whispered the word *California* with his dying breath.

# Chronology

**1813** John Charles Frémont is born January 21 in Savannah, Georgia, to French immigrant Charles Fremon (who eventually changes his name to Frémont) and Ann Whiting, whom Fremon later marries.

**1818** Charles Fremon dies; Ann Whiting Frémont purchases a boardinghouse to support herself while raising John and his three siblings.

**1827** John C. Frémont enrolls in Charleston College, South Carolina.

**1833** Serves as a mathematics teacher aboard the South America-bound U.S. Navy vessel *Natchez*; the experience aboard ship whets his taste for exploration.

**1838** Wins appointment as a second lieutenant in the U.S. Army Corps of Topographical Engineers.

**1841** Marries Jessie Benton, daughter of the powerful U.S. senator Thomas Hart Benton.

**1842** Leads his first expedition of the Oregon Trail as far west as the South Pass in Wyoming.

**1843** Explores a vast region composing Utah and Nevada as part of his second expedition into the Oregon Territory; names the region the Great Basin.

**1845** Newspaper editor John L. O'Sullivan first uses the term *Manifest Destiny*.

**1846** During his third exploration of the West, arrives in California and helps spark the Bear Flag Rebellion.

**1849** Fails to find a route through the Rocky Mountains for a western railroad line; the ill-fated wintertime crossing ends in the deaths of 10 men under his command.

**1850** Serves as one of the first U.S. senators from California

**1856** Runs for president as the first national candidate of the Republican Party; loses election to James Buchanan.

**1861** Appointed major general in the Union army by President Lincoln after the Civil War breaks out.

**1890** Dies in New York City on July 13.

# Glossary

**abolitionist**—a person in favor of doing away with, or abolishing, slavery.

**annex**—to take land belonging to another country and make it a part of one's own country.

**aristocrat**—a member of the highest or noble class.

**botanist**—a person who studies plants.

**cede**—to transfer land to another country, often by means of a treaty.

**chronometer**—an instrument for measuring time with great accuracy.

**conquistador**—a Spaniard who conquered American Indian peoples during the 16th century.

**contingent**—a detachment of soldiers or others organized for a specific duty.

**corps**—a group of people working together under the same commander.

**court-martial**—to try a member of the armed forces according to the rules of military justice.

**duel**—a formal combat between two persons, fought with weapons in the presence of witnesses.

**elope**—to run away secretly in order to get married without the permission of one's parents.

**guillotine**—an instrument for executing people by chopping off their heads, used especially in France during and after the French Revolution.

**homesteaders**–persons who settled on and worked lands in order to receive title to those lands.

**Manifest Destiny**–the idea, popular during the 1800s, that the United States was meant to expand its borders to the Pacific Ocean.

**manuscript**–a written work before it is published.

**pension**–a fixed sum, granted by a government as a favor or reward, that is paid regularly.

**regiment**–a large military unit.

**secede**–to withdraw from a political organization, state, or country.

**sextant**–an instrument for determining latitude and longitude.

**topography**–the art of mapping the natural features, including mountains, of a region.

**tributaries**–streams that flow into larger rivers or lakes.

# Further Reading

Green, Carl A., and William R. Sanford. *John C. Frémont: Soldier and Pathfinder*. Hillside, N.J.: Enslow Publishers, 1996.

Gudde, Erwin G., and Elizabeth K. Gudde, eds. *Exploring with Frémont: The Private Diaries of Charles Preuss*. Norman: University of Oklahoma Press, 1958.

Harris, Edward D. *John Charles Frémont and the Great Western Reconnaissance*. New York: Chelsea House Publishers, 1990.

Phillips, Catherine Coffin. *Jessie Benton Frémont: A Woman Who Made History*. Lincoln: University of Nebraska Press, 1995.

Roberts, David. *A Newer World: Kit Carson, John C. Frémont, and the Claiming of the American West*. Carmichael, Calif.: Touchstone Books, 2001.

Syme, Ronald. *John Charles Frémont, The Last American Explorer*. New York: William Morrow and Co., 1974.

Ward, John William. *Andrew Jackson—Symbol for an Age*. London: Oxford University Press, 1955.

# Picture Credits

**HAL MARCOVITZ** is a reporter for the *Allentown (Pa.)
Morning Call.* His work for Chelsea House includes biographies of explorers Marco Polo, John Smith, and Francisco
Vazquez de Coronado; the Indian guide Sacagawea; and the
Apollo astronauts. He lives in Chalfont, Pennsylvania, with his
wife, Gail, and daughters, Ashley and Michelle.